C_TS422

SAP S/4HANA Production Planning and Manufacturing

Table of Contents

Topic Areas

Introduction to SAP S/4HANA Supply Chain Planning < 10%

Introduction to SAP S/4HANA Production Planning < 10%

Demand Management < 10%

Advanced Planning - 11 to 20 %

Capacity Planning < 10%

Lean Manufacturing < 10%

Master Data 21 to 30 %

Production Orders 11 to 30 %

Material Requirements Planning < 10%

Process Orders < 10%

Description

The certification test SAP Certified Application Associate-SAP S/4HANA Production Planning and Manufacturing confirms that the applicant possesses the essential and foundational knowledge in extended warehouse management needed for the consultant position. This certification attests to the candidate's general comprehension and practical application of the information in projects, enabling them to successfully contribute to the planning and execution stages in a mentored capacity.

About Certification

Level	Associate
Exam	80 questions
Pass Score	65%
Duration	180 mins

150+ Scenario based practice exam questions and Answers of C_TS422 SAP Certified Application Associate - SAP S/4HANA Production Planning and Manufacturing exam.

Note: Correct answers are marked in BOLD. This assessment includes multiple choice and multiple response questions. For single choice questions, select one single answer. For multiple response questions, select more than one answer (the number of correct answers is stated in the question).

Disclaimer

These questions are for self-evaluation purposes and may or may not appear on the actual certification exams. Answering these questions correctly is no guarantee that you will pass the certification exam. The certification exam tries covers a much broader spectrum of topics, so do make sure you have familiarized yourself with all topics listed in the exam competency areas before taking the certification exam. This book will help you in preparation of certification exam.

One Correct Answer Questions

Q1. To trigger a goods receipt posting, which Kanban status do you have to set?

Ans:

- A. In use
- B. Empty
- **C. Full**
- D. Wait

Q2. A material in your company is planned with planning strategy 70 (Planning at assembly level). The consumption mode has been set to backward with a consumption period of 12 days. Starting from when are the 12 days counted backwards?

Ans:

- A. From the availability date of the related finished good
- B. From the planned independent requirement date of the material
- **C. From the dependent requirement date of the material**
- D. From the requested delivery date of the related finished good

Q3. What generates capacity requirements in a process order?

Ans:

- A. Relationships
- **B. Phases**
- C. Operations
- D. Resources

Q4. You run MRP for a material that was planned using Demand-Driven Replenishment. Toward which buffer level does the MRP run create a replenishment proposal?

Ans:

- **A. Top of Green**

B. Top of Red

C. Top of Yellow

D. Top of Red Base

Q5. Which transaction code can you use in SAP S/4HANA to enter and display goods movements?

Ans:

A. MBNL

B. MMBE

C. MB02

D. MIGO

Q6. In which data object is the production line (Repetitive manufacturing relevant work center) maintained?

Ans:

A. Bill of material

B. Cost collector

C. Production version

D. Repetitive manufacturing profile

Q7. What is the first step in the MRP run?

Ans:

A. Source determination

B. BOM explosion

C. Lot size calculation

D. Net requirements calculation

Q8. Your project uses process orders for the production of liquid chemicals. What can you define to ensure that the production flow happens only in physically connected tanks?

Ans:

   A. Setup matrix
   B. Operation network
   C. Resource network
   D. **Work center hierarchy**

Q9. The setup time on the production line to produce material is extensive. You would like to avoid multiple setups and limit the production of the material based on a planning calendar. Which type of lot size procedure should you use to accomplish this?

Ans:

   A. Minimum lot sizing
   B. Fixed lot sizing
   C. **Periodic lot sizing**
   D. Exact lot sizing

Q10. Your quality department detects a deviation in a raw material batch. Unfortunately, this batch has already been used in production. How can you identify all affected finished goods stocks?

Ans:

   A. Use the material staging report.
   B. **Use the batch information cockpit.**
   C. Use the material where-used report.
   D. Use batch determination.

Q11. How is the bill of material (BOM) exploded when you use a BOM explosion number?

Ans:

    A. With respect to a common change status for product and each assembly

    B. With respect to a defined separate change status for product and each assembly

    C. With respect to defined separate key dates for product and each assembly

    D. With respect to a common key date for product and each assembly

Q12. How is the bill of material (BOM) exploded when you use a BOM explosion number?

Ans:

    A. With respect to a common key date for the product and each assembly

    B. With respect to defined separate change status for the product and each assembly

    C. With respect to defined separate key dates for product and each assembly

    D. With respect to common change status for the product and each assembly

Q13. In the Manage Shortage view of the new SAP Fiori app "Monitor Material Coverage", what do the stars indicate?

Ans:

    A. The priority of the proposed solution

    B. The presence of production orders

    C. The viability of the proposed solution

    D. The presence of firmed planned orders

Q14. Which of the following functions can be performed when the production order has the status "Created" (CRTD)?

Ans:

    A. A user trigger material availability check via mass processing (transaction COHV)

    B. A user can trigger material staging via mass processing (transaction COHV).

    C. A user trigger printing of shop floor paper manually (transaction CO02).

D. A user can schedule a background job to release production orders (transaction COOIS).

Q15. The procurement type of your material is set to "E" for In-house production. Which of the following is valid to determine a source of supply in SAP S/4HANA?
Ans:

A. Production Version
B. Purchasing Info Record
C. Selection Method
D. Contract

Q16. Which data object can be updated with the scheduling results of a routing?
Ans:

A. Material master
B. MRP profile
C. Production scheduling profile
D. Production version

Q17. To ensure that the warehouse operator only stages large components in the exact required quality for each production order, which warehouse material staging method would you recommend?
Ans:

A. Pick parts
B. Crate parts
C. Release order parts
D. Kanban

Q18. A planner updated a production order status from partially confirmed "PCNF" to technically completed "TECO" by mistake. What impact would this have to other users for this specific production order?

Ans:

A. **The production operator cannot enter additional confirmations**

B. The production manager can still see the capacity requirements

C. The warehouse clerk still carry out goods issue transactions

D. The buyer can still see component reservations

Q19. Which process order function uses resource network?

Ans:

A. **Resource Selection**

B. resource scheduling

C. Capacity levelling

D. Capacity planning

Q20. In which customizing activity do you set up automatic routing selection for production orders?

Ans:

A. **Define order-type-dependent parameter**

B. Define scheduling parameters for production orders

C. Define production scheduling profile

D. Define selection profiles

Q21. A resource was created in SAP S/4HANA PP/DS through the internal CIF integration and named "W1904_1000_001". What does the suffix 001 in the resource name represent?

Ans:

A. **Capacity category**

B. Work center category

C. Number of individual capacities

D. Available capacity version

Q22. How can Production Planning and Detailed Scheduling (PP/DS) enhance the standard planning functionality?

Ans:

A. **By providing replenishment proposals with exact times**

B. By providing cross-plant planning and deployment

C. By providing future demands from demand figures in the past

D. By providing multilevel material requirements planning

Q23. In a first step you have created master recipes. In which sequence are the additional objects created?

Ans:

A. Process order, Control recipe, Process message, PI sheet

B. **Process order, Control recipe, PI sheet, Process message**

C. Process message, Control recipe, Process order, Process message

D. PI sheet, Control recipe, Process order, PI sheet

Q24. How can you limit the number of master data objects to be created when the manufacturing process is the same for many different products?

Ans:

A. By assigning the same production version to different materials

B. By creating routings with alternative sequences

C. **By assigning different materials to the same routing**

D. By creating routings with parallel sequences

Q25. What does the bill of material usage (BOM usage) control at the BOM item level?

Ans:

    A. Default unit of measure

    B. Maximum allowed low-level code

    C. Allowed material type

    D. Default values for the item status

Q26. Which Kanban master data object controls the relationship between the supply and demand source?

Ans:

    A. Kanban-container

    B. Production supply area

    C. Control cycle

    D. Rate routing

Q27. Which of the following is used by the MRP Live planning run in SAP S/4HANA?

Ans:

    A. Parallel processing across servers

    B. Net change planning

    C. Planning horizon

    D. MRP list

Q28. A planner wants to interactively resolve an overload situation on a resource using advanced planning tools without any automatic rescheduling activity by the system. Which combination of settings for resource and detailed scheduling strategy are required to receive related alerts?

Ans:

    A. Finite resource and infinite strategy

    B. Infinite resource and finite strategy

    C. Infinite resource and infinite strategy

D. Finite resource and finite strategy

Q29. You produce your material based on a forecast derived from historical sales and expect it to be in inventory when your customer orders. If customers order more that the forecasted quantity, you want to increase production to try to meet the extra demand. Which is the appropriate planning strategy to use?

Ans:

A. 10 - Anonymous make-to-stock

B. 50 - Planning without final assembly

C. 40 - Planning with-final-assembly

D. 20 - Make to order production

Q30. Which of the following data objects are updated when a user confirms an operation?

Ans:

A. Shop floor information system

B. Production order header status

C. Production order total order quantity

D. Warehouse transfer order status

Q31. Which of the following is an advantage of MRP Live and NOT available in classical MRP?

Ans:

A. MRP Live can priorities demand from sales orders

B. MRP Live can plan materials with recursive BOMs

C. MRP Live can propose alternative solutions

D. MRP Live can create production orders automatically

Q32. In order to use strategy 70 - Planning At Assembly Level, what order field must be set besides the planning strategy?

Ans:

    A. Dependent Requirements indicator

    B. Storage Location MRP Indicator

    C. Individual/Collective Indicator

    D. Mixed MRP indicator

Q33. The pegging situation was changed from an MRP heuristic run. What is a capability of dynamic pegging?

Ans:

    A. It propagates changed sales order priorities to the pegged planned orders.

    B. It replaces fixed pegging relationships unless they have been created for stock.

    C. It links receipts from an alternative location in case of a shortage in the default location.

    D. It enables the propagation of network alerts across the bill of materials structure.

Q34. You are using heuristic SAP MRP 001. Which of the following criteria are included in the automatic source determination logic when a planned order is created?

Ans:

    A. Component availability

    B. Quota arrangement

    C. Delivery date

    D. Vendor rating

Q35. In a production process, you need a certain amount of liquid as input material. The source tank is directly connected to the reactor. How can you process consumption postings?

Ans:

A. Backflushing

B. Picking list

C. Kanban

D. Transfer Order

Q36. What are the consequences if operation status Dispatched is set for a production order operation?

Ans:

A. You can reschedule the operation using lead the scheduling.

B. You can reschedule the operation using finite Scheduling in a planning board.

C. You can reschedule the order using material requirements planning.

D. You can reschedule the order using lead time scheduling.

Q37. What does a line hierarchy in repetitive manufacturing represent?

Ans:

A. A production line with a parallel sequence in the routing

B. A production line with an alternative sequence in the routing

C. A production line with prioritized alternative work centers

D. A production line with more than one work center

Q38. What is the correct sequence of the following Activate methodology phases?

Ans:

A. Prepare, Validate, Test, Go-Live

B. Prepare, Realize, Iterate, Continuous Improvement

C. Prepare, Explore, Realize, Deploy

D. Validate, Perform, Test, Deploy

Q39. What do you use to schedule operations from planned orders so that the production plan can be fulfilled?

Ans:

    A. Material Requirements Planning (MRP)

    B. Supply Network Planning (SNP)

    C. Demand Planning (DP)

    D. Capacity Requirements Planning (CRP)

Q40. For what production type are production orders used?

Ans:

    A. Discrete manufacturing processes

    B. Replenishment controlled by control cycles

    C. Period and quantity-oriented production

    D. Process manufacturing processes

Q41. Which of the following is a valid sequence of the main activities in product on order processing?

Ans:

    A. Creation, staging, release, material withdrawal, confirmation.

    B. Creation, release, scheduling, material withdrawal, confirmation.

    C. Creation, scheduling, release, material withdrawal, confirmation.

    D. Creation, scheduling, release, variance calculation, confirmation.

Q42. You want to reduce planning efforts for B/C materials. Which planning procedure do you recommend?

Ans:

    A. Forecast planning

    B. Material requirements planning

    C. Manual planning without check

D. **Consumption-based planning**

Q43. You want to triggering-house production of a semi-finished mater al before a sales order for the corresponding finished good is received. Which planning strategy supports the consumption of planned independent requirements for the semi-finished material?
Ans:
   A. Planning with final assembly (40)
   B. Make-to-order production (20)
   C. **Planning without final assembly (50)**
   D. Planning at assembly level (70)

Q44. A material has been set up as a phantom assembly by entering the special procurement key in the material master. How can you switch off the phantom assembly in a specific bill of material(BOM)?
Ans:
   A. **Change the explosion type of the phantom assembly in the BOM.**
   B. Change the special procurement key of the phantom assembly in the BOM.
   C. Change the phantom item indicator for the phantom assembly in the BOM.
   D. Change the item category of the phantom assembly in the BOM.

Q45. You are working with planning strategy 40 (Planning-with-final assembly). When does consumption of planned independent requirements take place?
Ans:
   A. When the MRP results are saved
   B. When you create a planned order
   C. **When you create a sales order**
   D. When you deliver a sales order

Q46. You use planning strategy Finite Scheduling - with Reverse and want to allow scheduling in the past. How can you achieve this?

Ans:

    A. Specify a negative planning horizon in the strategy profile.

    B. Specify a positive offset time in the strategy profile.

    C. Specify a negative offset time in the strategy profile.

    D. Specify a positive planning horizon in the strategy profile.

Q47. Your project uses process orders for the production of liquid chemicals. What can you define to ensure that the production flow happens only in physically connected tanks?

Ans:

    A. Setup matrix

    B. Work center hierarchy

    C. Resource network

    D. Operation network

Q48. You want to integrate an existing planned order into Advanced Production Planning. Which report do you use?

Ans:

    A. /SAPAPO/PPDS_DELTA_ORD_TRANS

    B. /SAPAPO/CREATE_LOCATION

    C. /SAPAPO/CURTO_CREATE

    D. /SAPAPO/UPD_LOC_SP_PL

Q49. You have a quality control check to avoid using a high-value component tin faulty materials in subsequent assembly operations. How do you account for potential scrap of the high value material?

Ans:

A. Enter the component scrap in the component of the bill of material of the assembly and leave the net indicator initial in the bill of material.
B. Enter the assembly scrap in the material master of the component and set the net indicator in the component of the bill of material of the assembly.
C. Enter the component scrap in the material master of the assembly and set the net indicator in the routing operation where V D the component is used.
D. Enter the operation scrap and set the net indicator in the component of the bill of material of the assembly.

Q50. When working with both cross-plant and plant-specific material statuses in the material master, which status has the highest priority?
Ans:
A. The plant-specific status
B. The most restrictive status
C. The least restrictive status
D. The cross-plant status

Q51. What new technology is used in SAP S/4HANA Embedded Analytics? Please choose the correct answer.
Ans:
A. HANA Live
B. Smart Business Cockpit
C. ABAP Managed Core Data Services (CDS)
D. Multidimensional Reporting client (MDRC)

Q52. What does it mean for the production planner when MRP works with infinite capacities?
Ans:

A. MRP creates capacity requirements only if the work center has sufficient capacity.

B. MRP assigns capacity requirements automatically after the last scheduled order on a work center.

C. MRP creates capacity requirements without checking the capacity of a work center.

D. MRP assigns capacity requirements automatically to work center is with the earliest available capacity.

Q53. Which material master setting is required to use the repetitive planning table for production with production orders?

Ans:

A. An overall profile be assigned on the Work Scheduling view

B. A repetitive manufacturing profile must be assigned on the MRP4 view

C. The Selection Method must be set to "2 Selection by production version"

D. At least one valid production version must exist on the MRP4 view

Q54. The procurement type of your material is set to "E" for In-house production. Which of the following is valid to determine a source of supply in SAP S/4HANA? Please choose the correct answer.

Ans:

A. Purchasing Info Record.

B. Production Version.

C. Contract.

D. Selection Method.

Q55. In your project, you have several materials that are planned by different people. How can you assign the planning responsibility?

Ans:

A. MRP group

B. MRP controller

C. MRP type

D. MRP planning file

Q56. What are the consequences if operation status Dispatched is set for a production order operation?

Ans:

A. You can reschedule the order using lead time scheduling.

B. You can reschedule the operation using lead the scheduling.

C. You can reschedule the operation using finite Scheduling in a planning board.

D. You can reschedule the order using material requirements planning.

Q57. What is the difference between co-products and by-products?

Ans:

A. Only co-products are identified by a special item category in the bill of material (BOM).

B. Only co-products appear in the process or production order settlement rule.

C. Only by-products have a zero-inventory valuation.

D. Only co-products can be manufactured in isolation from the main product.

Q58. What must be used in the system to plan the requirements for different subcontractors separately?

Ans:

A. Production versions.

B. MRP areas.

C. Storage locations.

D. Planning plant.

Q59. When do you use variant bills of materials (BOMB)?

Ans:

    A. When a material has multiple BOMB.

    B. When multiple material is have similar BOMB.

    C. When multiple material also have the same BOM.

    D. When a material has a configurable BOM.

Q60. What is a work center hierarchy in SAP S/4HANA capacity planning?

Ans:

    A. A group of work centers in a parallel sequence that is used to split product on quantities and work on them in parallel.

    B. A group of alternative work centers providing a cumulative available capacity for production.

    C. A group of work centers in a production line being used in sequence for production.

    D. A group of alternative work centers for production, structured in hierarchy levels by prior ties.

Q61. What determines whether the planned independent requirements in MRP consume other requirements?

Ans:

    A. Requirements type

    B. Requirements profile

    C. Order type

    D. Consumption sequence procedure

Q62. When analyzing the SAP ECC order report for a planned order for a finished product, you discover that one of the assemblies will not be available in time for the scheduled final assembly because of automatic forward scheduling. Which planning procedure do you use to create a feasible production plan from a requirements planning perspective?

Ans:

- A. Total planning online
- B. Multi-level single-item planning with the "simulation mode" option
- C. Interactive single-item planning for the delayed assembly
- **D. Multi-level single-item planning with the "display material list" option**

Q63. Which document is skipped when SAP EWM is embedded in SAP S/4HANA?

Ans:

- A. Warehouse task
- B. Outbound delivery order
- **C. Outbound delivery request**
- D. Warehouse order

Q64. What is SAP's strategic solution to perform Sales and Operations planning when you use SAP S/4HANA Manufacturing?

Ans:

- **A. Integrated Business Planning**
- B. APO Demand Planning
- C. PP Standard Sales and Operations Planning
- D. Flexible Planning

Q65. In the Manage Shortage view of the new SAP Fiori app "Monitor Material Coverage', what do the stars indicate?

Ans:

A. The presence of production orders

B. The presence of signed planned orders

C. The priority of the proposed solution

D. **The viability of the proposed solution**

Q66. You want to procure your material components based on a forecast for the finished material derived from historical sales. When customers order, you produce the finished product and reserve it for that particular order. Which is the appropriate planning strategy to use?

Ans:

A. 20 Make-to-order production

B. **50 Planning without final assembly**

C. 40 Planning with final assembly

D. 30 Production by lot size

Q67. You select the master data for production orders via production versions. Which information is contained in a production version?

Ans:

A. The explosion dates for the routing and BOM

B. The control parameters for selecting routings and BOM

C. The default order type to be used

D. **The routing and BOM alternatives to be used**

Q68. In Make-to-order production, which field controls whether the components will be planned as sales order specific stock?

Ans:

A. The item category of the component in the BOM

B. **The Planning Strategy of the finished product**

C. The MRP Type of the component

D. The Individual/Collective indicator of the component

Q69. Which property applies for consumption with planning strategy 40 (planning with final assembly)?

Ans:

A. Consumption can reduce the total originally planned production quantity.

B. Consumption creates a static and binding assignment between the planned independent requirements and the customer requirements for the entire procurement process.

C. Consumption takes place with the planning material.

D. Consumption can increase the total originally planned production quantity.

Q70. At the end of the MRP run you receive the exception message "Reschedule In Operation". What caused the message to be generated?

Ans:

A. The requirement no longer exists

B. The requirements date occurs that of a signed planned receipt

C. A signed planned receipt cannot be rescheduled

D. The requirements date occurs before that of a signed planned receipt.

Two Correct Answers Questions

Q71. Which supply chain planning components can you find in SAP S/4HANA? Note: There are 2 correct answers to this question.

Ans:

    A. Advanced Planning

    B. Supply Network Planning

    C. Supply Chain Control Tower

    D. Capacity Requirements Planning

Q72. Which material master data can you copy when you use the Copy Material program (transaction MMCC, Material Master Copier) to create new materials? Note: There are 2 correct answers to this question.

Ans:

    A. Storage location data

    B. Warehouse number data

    C. MRP area data

    D. Production version data

Q73. Which of the following elements does the MRP run take into account? Note: There are 2 correct answers to this question.

Ans:

    A. Sales orders

    B. Planned independent requirements

    C. Shipments

    D. Material documents

Q74. Advanced Planning is delivered with standard out-of-the-box order and resource evaluations. Which evaluations are available? Note: There are 2 correct answers to this question.

Ans:

- A. Resource overview
- B. **Resource utilization**
- C. **Order list**
- D. Production list

Q75. Which options are available for an SAP S/4HANA deployment? Note: There are 2 correct answers to this question.

Ans:

- A. SAP S/4HANA Professional services cloud
- B. **SAP S/4HANA private cloud**
- C. **SAP S/4HANA on premise**
- D. SAP S/4AHANA Enterprise Management cloud

Q76. What does the bill of material usage (BOM usage) control at the BOM item level? Note: There are 2 correct answers to this question.

Ans:

- A. **Default values for the item status**
- B. **Allowed material type**
- C. Default unit of measure
- D. Maximum allowed low-level code

Q77. Which of the following objects can you release so that the business transactions for process order execution and process management can be executed? Note: There are 2 correct answers to this question.

Ans:

A. Individual control recipes

B. Individual phases

C. Individual process instructions

D. Individual operations

Q78. Which task list types can have parallel sequences? Note: There are 2 correct answers to this question.

Ans:

A. Master recipes

B. Rate routings (R)

C. Routings (N)

D. Reference operation sets

Q79. How can you carry out cost object controlling for production orders? Note: There are 2 correct answers to this question.

Ans:

A. Product-related

B. Milestone-related

C. Cost-related

D. Order-related

Q80. The SAP Kanban procedure could be used to trigger which of the following kinds of replenishment? Note: There are 2 correct answers to this question.

Ans:

A. In-house production

B. Subcontracting

C. Stock transfer

D. Seller consignment

Q81. What could be the reason for multiple commitment of individual capacities, where several operations have the same scheduled dates on a resource after capacity planning? Note: There are 2 correct answers to this question.

Ans:

    A. Alternative resources are fully occupied.

    B. The planning strategy is infinite.

    C. The Change Planning Direct on indicator is set.

    D. The work center has several individual capacities.

Q82. When would you use reporting point backflush in repetitive manufacturing? Note: There are 2 correct answers to this question.

Ans:

    A. You require an up-to-date inventory for components

    B. For production lines with short lead times

    C. When you need to determine the work in progress

    D. When goods issues can wait for final confirmation

Q83. A warehouse manager likes to streamline the goods receipt (GR) process for production orders. Where can you enable the automatic GR? Note: There are 2 correct answers to this question.

Ans:

    A. Operation control key

    B. Confirmation profile

    C. Production scheduling profile

    D. Scheduling margin key

Q84. The production plan is being disrupted by last minute demands that are entered in the system. Which is the most efficient way to handle last minute demands and protect the current production plan? Note: There are 2 correct answers to this question.

Ans:

A. Manually firm all planned orders for materials within the replenishment lead time of the material.

B. In the stock requirements list, set a manual firming fence for a date based on the replenishment lead time of the material.

C. In the material master record, set MRP type to P4 and a planning time fence on the replenishment lead time of the material.

D. In the material master record, set MRP type to P1 and a planning time fence on the replenishment lead time of the material.

Q85. On which of the following levels can you influence the availability check for the components of production orders? Note: There are 2 correct answers to this question.

Ans:

A. Production controller

B. Production order type

C. MRP-controller

D. Master material

Q86. How can you avoid order proposals for planned independent requirements with dates in the past? Note: There are 2 correct answers to this question.

Ans:

A. Set the requirements reduction indicator in the requirements class

B. Reorganize planned independent requirements

C. Use a planning strategy with consumption requirements

D. Maintain adjustment parameter in the MRP group

Q87. Where can you maintain consumption mode and consumption periods for planning strategies? Note: There are 2 correct answers to this question.

Ans:

A. In the requirements class

B. In the plant parameters

C. In the MRP group

D. In the material master

Q88. For which data objects do you have to set up CIF integration models in S/4HANA to use them in advanced planning? Note: There are 2 correct answers to this question.
Ans:

A. Material master

B. Production plant

C. Work center

D. Contract

Q89. You want to perform capacity availability checks on your production orders. What must be set for this to occur? Note: There are 2 correct answers to this question.
Ans:

A. Indicator Relevant for finite scheduling must be set.

B. Checking rule and group must be assigned.

C. Checking control must have an overall profile assigned in customizing.

D. PRT Availability check must be set.

Q90. For which planning-relevant data objects do you set just one indicator to include then in PP/DS? Note: There are 2 correct answers to this question.
Ans:

A. Plant

B. Material

C. Work center

D. Production version

Q91. What capabilities does SAP S/4HANA embedded analytics provide? Note: There are 2 correct answers to this question.

Ans:

    A. Automatic update of story boards

    B. Comparison of current data with historical data to identify trends

    C. Strategic analysis

    D. Real time decision support

Q92. What are properties of MRP Live? Note: There are 2 correct answers to this question.

Ans:

    A. It is executed on the database server

    B. The code is written in SQL Script

    C. Data is read sequentially from the database tables

    D. It uses the same BAdis as classic MRP

Q93. The material master of your finished product contains MRP type "PD". You set a manual firming date in the stock requirements list. Which of the following will sign planned orders"? Note: There are 2 correct answers to this question.

Ans:

    A. Setting a planning time fence in the Material Master Record

    B. Creating a planned order within the planning time fence

    C. Assigning a production scheduling profile

    D. Manually changing the quantity of a planned order

Q94. The production plan is being disrupted by last minute demands that are entered in the system. Which is the most efficient way to handle last minute demands and protect the current production plan? Note: There are 2 correct answers to this question.

Ans:

A. **In the stock requirements list, set a manual firming fence for a date based on the replenishment lead time of the material**

B. In the material master record, set MRP type to PI and a planning time fence on the replenishment lead time of the material

C. In the material master record, set MRP type to P4 and a planning time fence on the replenishment lead time of the material

D. **Manually sign all planned orders for materials within the replenishment lead time of the material**

Q95. A customer is considering switching from order-related settlement to product-related settlement. What are capabilities of cost collectors? Note: There are 2 correct answers to this question.

Ans:

A. **They can be applied to make-to-stock production order.**

B. They can be used for manufacturing with collective orders.

C. They can be created automatically during month end process.

D. **They can be used for repetitive manufacturing.**

Q96. Which functional capabilities does the Detailed Scheduling Board have? Note: There are 2 correct answers to this question.

Ans:

A. **Undo for drag & drop planning activities**

B. Enter time-ticket confirmation for production orders

C. **Change planned order quantities**

D. Change sales order quantities

Q97. When the goods receipt for a finished product is posted during confirmation in a repetitive manufacturing environment, which of the following actions are also performed by default? Note: There are 2 correct answers to this question.

Ans:

- **A. Reduction of the capacity requirements**
- B. Staging of components for the next order in the sequence
- C. Archiving of backflush documents
- **D. Posting of production costs to cost collector**

Q98. You want to create a production order from a planned order. What methods could you

use? Note: There are 2 correct answers to this question.

Ans:

- **A. Full conversion**
- **B. Partial conversion**
- C. Individual conversion
- D. Order release

Q99. In which, material master views can you select the batch management checkbox? There are 2 correct answers to this question.

Ans:

- **A. Purchasing**
- **B. Work Scheduling**
- C. Basic Data 1
- D. MRP 4

Q100. When can the material availability check occur automatically in a production order? Note: There are 2 correct answers to this question.

Ans:

- **A. At order creation**
- **B. At order release**
- C. At order settlement

D. At order confirmation

Q101. What is the purpose of a reporting point confirmation in repetitive manufacturing? Note: There are 2 correct answers to this question.

Ans:

A. **To determine the work in progress along the production line**
B. **To provide timely updates of inventory management for the staged components**
C. To stage different components for a production line simultaneously
D. To reduce the total production lead time for along production line

Q102. What are some uses for the low-level code assigned to each material? Note: There are 2 correct answers to this question.

Ans:

A. It is used by ATP to determine the priority of alternative components.
B. It is used by engineering to identify sub items in an engineering bill of material(BOM).
C. **It is used in MRP to determine the sequence in which materials are planned.**
D. **It is used by product costing to determine how costs are rolled up.**

Q103. Advanced Planning uses master data and transaction data from SAP S/4HANA In which data object can you set the advanced planning flag? Note: There are 2 correct answers to this question.

Ans:

A. **Material**
B. Production version
C. Plant
D. **Work center**

Q104. You have a scheduling agreement with a vendor. You want classic MRP to automatically create schedule lines in case of material shortage. What must you do? Note: There are 2 correct answers to this question.

Ans:

- A. Add the agreement to the quota arrangement and mark it for MRP relevance.
- **B. Add the agreement to the source list and mark it for MRP relevance.**
- C. Set the creation indicator for purchase requisitions on the initial screen of the MRP run.
- **D. Set the creation indicator for delivery schedule lines on the initial screen of the MRP run.**

Q105. Which bill of material (BOM) categories can you define in SAP S/4HANA? Note: There are 2 correct answers to this question.

Ans:

- **A. Functional Location BOM**
- B. Work Center BOM
- **C. Sales Order BOM**
- D. Class BOM

Q106. What data can you maintain in the sub items of a bill of material (BOM)? Note: There are 2 correct answers to this question.

Ans:

- A. Scrap percentage
- B. Item type
- **C. Installation point**
- **D. Quantity**

Q107. Your client is asking for your advice on material master numbering in SAP S/4HANA. What do you need to consider? Note: There are 2 correct answers to this question.

Ans:

A. **The maximum mater all number length is 40 for external numbers and 18 for internal numbers.**

B. In Customizing you can decide by material type whether to use the long material number.

C. **The display template for material numbers applies to all clients.**

D. The number of leading zeros for internal numbers is client specific.

Q108. In which data objects do you maintain the production line as the work center for repetitive manufacturing? Note: There are 2 correct answers to this question.

Ans:

A. Repetitive manufacturing profile

B. Production cost collector

C. **Production version**

D. **Routing**

Q109. You need to model goods receipt processing time in Detailed Scheduling. Which modelling options do you have? Note: There are 2 correct answers to this question.

Ans:

A. Model a separate resource in the production data structure.

B. Model a resource inbound in the location master.

C. **Model a transportation resource in the location master.**

D. **Model a handling resource in the location master and goods receipt time in the mater all master.**

Q110. Which chart types does the tabular planning table provide in SAP S/4HANA? Note: There are 2 correct answers to this question.

Ans:

    A. Orders (dispatched) chart

    B. Capacity requirements chart

    C. Work center capacities chart

    D. Order (pool) chart

Q111. What does the industry sector determine? Note: There are 2 correct answers to this question.

Ans:

    A. Which material master views can be maintained

    B. Which transaction you can use to create a new material

    C. Whether material numbers are assigned internally or externally

    D. Whether a material master field is required, changeable, displayed, or hidden

Q112. How can you limit the validity of a bill of material (BOM)? Note: There are 2 correct answers to this question.

Ans:

    A. By industry

    B. By period

    C. By plant

    D. By material type

Q113. What are some of the advantages of using Kanban? Note: There are 2 correct answers to this question.

Ans:

    A. It is a simplified form of production control

B. It is mostly accomplished by manual postings

C. Replenishments are created close to the actual need

D. Replenishments are based on centralized planning

Q114. Which time elements are relevant for lead t me scheduling of a product on order? Note: There are 2 correct answers to this question.

Ans:

A. Setup time

B. Float after production

C. Total replenishment lead time

D. Planned delivery time

Q115. You are using the document management system (DMS). Where should the DMS document links be assigned, to have them automatically copied to production orders. Note: There are 2 correct answers to this question.

Ans:

A. Bill of material

B. Work center

C. Routing header

D. Material master

Q116. You have maintained planning strategy group 10 (make-to-stock production) in the material master of a material. For the coming months, you have planned requirements with requirement type LSF (derived from main strategy 10). Now, you want to change the requirement type from LSF to VSF (in accordance with planning strategy 40, planning with final assembly) for requirements in the existing production plan. Which of the following scenarios are applicable in this case? Note: There are 2 correct answers to this question.

Ans:

A. You can enter the strategy group 40 in the material master, but the requirement type is not changed automatically for existing requirements.

B. You can change the strategy group from 10 to 40 for the existing production plan in the material master, and the requirement type for all requirements is changed automatically.

C. You must change the requirement type for planning strategy 10 to VSF in Customizing. The requirement type for all existing requirements is then changed by the next planning run.

D. You can enter the strategy group 40 in the material master and change the present requirement for the product manually in the production plan.

Q117. What are the Pillars of SAP Activate? Note: There are 2 correct answers to this question.

Ans:

A. Premium engagement

B. Guided Configuration

C. SAP Max Attention

D. SAP Best Practices

Q118. Your customer wants to include restricted-use stock as a potential receipt in the existing ATP check for component availability. Which information is required to implement this change request in the scope of check? Note: There are 2 correct answers to this question.

Ans:

A. The ATP category for restricted-use stock

B. The checking rule from the business application

C. The checking group from the material master

D. The checking control for the order type

Q119. When modeling in-house production on which business levels can you create a bill of material (BOM)? Note: There are 2 correct answers to this question.

Ans:

    A. At the plant level

    B. At the company code level

    C. At the business area level

    D. At the client level

Three Correct Answers Questions

Q120. You are creating a production order manually. What activities are involved in this process? Note: There are 3 correct answers to this question.

Ans:

    A. Planning selection

    B. Master data selection

    C. Capacity requirements determination

    D. Order type determination

    E. Actual cost calculation

Q121. Which of the following processes lead to an entry in the MRP planning file? Note: There are 3 correct answers to this question.

Ans:

    A. Creation of a purchasing contract

    B. Change of the storage bin

    C. Change of the material's procurement type

    D. Creation of a sales order

    E. Creation of dependent requirements

Q122. Which SAP solutions support the supplier area in the portfolio of the Digital Value Network? Note: There are 3 correct answers to this question.

Ans:

    A. SAP Concur

    B. SAP Field glass

    C. SAP SuccessFactors

    D. SAP C/4HANA

    E. SAP Ariba

Q123. In Demand-Driven Replenishment, materials are classified according to several criteria. What criteria can you use? Note: There are 3 correct answers to this question.

Ans:

    A. **Demand variation**

    B. Average daily usage

    C. Minimum order quantity

    D. **Usage in bill of materials**

    E. **Goods issue value**

Q124. What does forecasting in the demand planning cycle include? Note: There are 3 correct answers to this question.

Ans:

    A. Past quotation quantities

    B. **Past sales order quantities**

    C. **One-off events**

    D. **Market intelligence**

    E. Past procurement quantities

Q125. Which actions does the system perform by default when you save a confirmation for a finished product in repetitive manufacturing? Note: There are 3 correct answers to this question.

Ans:

    A. Material staging for next order in sequence

    B. **Reduction of associated capacity requirements**

    C. **Posting of production costs to the production cost collector**

    D. **Posting of goods receipt for the product**

    E. Archiving of documents for assembly scrap

Q126. What are attributes of the SAP S/4HANA Simplification list? Note: There are 3 correct answers to this question.

Ans:

    A. It details transaction and solution capabilities at a functional level

    B. It was created for better planning and estimation of your way to S/4HANA

    C. It can have a business and a technical impact

    D. It contains references to the relevant training material

    E. It is only a grouping of related technical simplifications

Q127. Which data model changes have been implemented in Sales and Distribution? Note: There are 3 correct answers to this question.

Ans:

    A. Elimination of status tables

    B. Elimination of output condition tables

    C. Elimination of customer master tables

    D. Elimination of LIS tables for rebates

    E. Elimination of document index tables

Q128. During planning you are facing an overload situation on a resource. Which activities do you consider to create a feasible production plan? Note: There are 3 correct answers to this question.

Ans:

    A. Use multilevel MRP run for the products on the resource

    B. Use a bucket-oriented capacity check

    C. Use rescheduling with an alternative mode

    D. Use DS heuristic "Schedule Sequence"

    E. Use optimization with respect to set-up times

Q129. What is the equivalent in SAP S/4HANA of the Production Data Structure in PP/DS? Note: There are 3 correct answers to this question.

Ans:

    A. **Bill of materials**

    B. **Routing**

    C. **Production Version**

    D. Engineering Change Record

Q130. Which automotive-specific functionality is embedded in SAP S/4HANA? Note: There are 3 correct answers to this question.

Ans:

    A. Equipment and Tools Management

    B. **Parts interchangeability**

    C. **Packaging Logistics**

    D. **Enhanced Kanban Processing**

    E. Enhanced characteristics-based processes

Q131. Which material-specific information can be transferred to a transportation lane in PP/DS? Note: There are 3 correct answers to this question.

Ans:

    A. Production versions

    B. **Outline agreement**

    C. **Special procurement keys**

    D. Quota arrangements

    E. **Purchasing info records**

Q132. What steps are possible in a PP/DS production planning run? Note: There are 3 correct answers to this question.

Ans:

A. Backorder processing

B. Optimization

C. Demand consumption

D. Heuristics

E. Detailed scheduling functions

Q133. Which of these are layers in SAP Best Practice content? Note: There are 3 correct answers to this question.

Ans:

A. Configuration guides

B. Process diagrams

C. Building blocks

D. Solution packages

E. Scope items

Q134. What are some of the SAP Fiori user types? Note: There are 3 correct answers to this question.

Ans:

A. Developer

B. Employee

C. Expert

D. Business partner

E. Occasional

Q135. Which time elements are part of a routing operation? Note: There are 3 correct answers to this question.

Ans:

A. Queue time

B. Wait time

C. Float before production

D. Pick/pack time

E. Move time

Q136. Your customer complains about the incorrect duration for production order operations. What time elements could cause the issue? Note: There are 3 correct answers to this question.

Ans:

A. Floating time

B. Queue time

C. Processing time

D. Move time

Q137. Which materials have a negative quantity in a bill of materials or in a recipe? Note: There are 3 correct answers to this question.

Ans:

A. Waste products

B. Continuous flow materials

C. By-products

D. Bulk materials

E. Co-products

Q138. How can you set up the supply source for the SAP Kanban process? Note: There are 3 correct answers to this question.

Ans:

A. Using quotations for internal and external procurement

B. Using purchasing costs for automated source prioritization

C. Using stock transfer reservations for stock transfer

D. Using run schedule quantities for in-house production

E. **Using purchase orders for external procurement**

Q139. How can you achieve a feasible production plan in case of capacity constraints? Note: There are 3 correct answers to this question.

Ans:

A. **Select an alternative mode on a resource.**

B. Reduce the planning window.

C. **Adjust the available capacity.**

D. Execute a new production planning run.

E. **Form optimum sequences to reduce setup times.**

Q140. What are the possible results of a production planning run in Advanced Planning (PP/OS)? Note: There are 3 correct answers to this question.

Ans:

A. **Planned order**

B. Stock transport order

C. **Purchase requisition**

D. Production order

E. **Scheduling agreement schedule line**

Q141. You are transferring data from SAP S/4HANAIo embedded PP/OS. What master data objects are mapped to a location? Note: There are 3 correct answers to this question.

Ans:

A. **Supplier**

B. **Plant**

C. Work center

D. **Customer**

Q142. What are possible configuration steps when setting up the alert monitor in Advanced Planning? Note: There are 3 correct answers to this question.

Ans:

    A. **Create object selection variant for product-related alerts.**

    B. **Assign the alert profile to the overall profile.**

    C. Create object selection variant for transportation lane-related alerts.

    D. **Create object selection variant for resource-related alerts**

    E. Assign the overall profile to the authorization profile.

Q143. Which of the following are capabilities of multidimensional reporting in SAP S/4HANA embedded analytics? Note: There are 3 correct answers to this question.

Ans:

    A. **Drill down**

    B. **Sort**

    C. Scheduling

    D. **Filters**

    E. Forecast

Q144. What are drawbacks of the separation of OLTP and OLAP? Note: There are 3 correct answers to this question.

Ans:

    A. **Multiple copies of the data exist**

    B. **Batch processes are required to keep OLTP and OLAP in sync**

    C. The OLAP system needs to write back the data to the OLTP system

    D. Only the OLAP system has the latest data

    E. **Only the OLAP system has a predefined subset of the data**

Q145. Which technological advances enabled the development of SAP S/4HANA as the digital core? Note: There are 3 correct answers to this question.

Ans:

A. **Big and affordable memory**

B. **Multi-core processors enabling parallelism of tasks**

C. Wide adoption of web standards such as Service-oriented architecture

D. **Capability to add to server landscape and scale**

E. Advances in the three-tier architecture approach

Q146. How does the new Inventory Management Data model contribute to the reduction of the data footprint? Note: There are 3 correct answers to this question.

Ans:

A. **By eliminating inventory tables**

B. By eliminating material master tables

C. **By eliminating inventory history tables**

D. **By eliminating fields for different stock types**

E. By eliminating hybrid tables

Q147. Which data model changes have been implemented in Sales and Distribution? Note: There are 3 correct answers to this question.

Ans:

A. **Elimination of customer master tables**

B. Elimination of LIS tables for rebates

C. Elimination of output condition tables

D. **Elimination of status tables**

E. **Elimination of document index tables**

Q148. Which warehouse management functions are available in SAP EWM but NOT in SAP WM? Note: There are 3 correct answers to this question.

Ans:

A. **Labor Management**

B. **Expected goods receipt**

C. Yard Management

D. Handling Unit Management

E. **Slotting**

Q149. Which advanced functionality has been embedded in SAP S/4HANA? Note: There are 3 correct answers to this question.

Ans:

A. Supply Network Planning

B. **Available-to-promise**

C. **Backorder processing**

D. **Capacity planning**

E. Demand planning

Q150. Before a user can add multiple production versions in a master material, what information should be collected? Note: There are 3 correct answers to this question.

Ans:

A. Work center hierarchy

B. **Lot sizes**

C. Task list group number

D. **Validity dates**

E. **BOM status**

Q151. Which elements are included in the structure of the batch where-used list? Note: There are 3 correct answers to this question.

Ans:

A. **Stock transfers**

B. Planned orders

C. **Transfers from batch to batch**

D. Collective orders

E. Purchase orders

Q152. What are the main innovations in manufacturing in SAP S/4HANA? Note: There are 3 correct answers to this question.

Ans:

A. Material Coverage Fiori app

B. Lock-free inventory movements

C. Rough-cut capacity planning

D. Flow manufacturing

E. Monitor Production Orders Fiori app

All the Best!